YOUR KNOWLEDGE HAS VALUE

Kelly Clarkson

Java and the Mobile Environment

GRIN Verlag

Bibliografische Information der Deutschen Nationalbibliothek:

Die Deutsche Bibliothek verzeichnet diese Publikation in der Deutschen National-
bibliografie; detaillierte bibliografische Daten sind im Internet über http://dnb.d-
nb.de/ abrufbar.

Imprint:

Copyright © 2012 GRIN Verlag GmbH
Druck und Bindung: Books on Demand GmbH, Norderstedt Germany
ISBN: 978-3-656-41447-6

This book at GRIN:

http://www.grin.com/en/e-book/213222/java-and-the-mobile-environment

GRIN - Your knowledge has value

Der GRIN Verlag publiziert seit 1998 wissenschaftliche Arbeiten von Studenten, Hochschullehrern und anderen Akademikern als eBook und gedrucktes Buch. Die Verlagswebsite www.grin.com ist die ideale Plattform zur Veröffentlichung von Hausarbeiten, Abschlussarbeiten, wissenschaftlichen Aufsätzen, Dissertationen und Fachbüchern.

Visit us on the internet:

http://www.grin.com/

http://www.facebook.com/grincom

http://www.twitter.com/grin_com

Java and the Mobile Environment

Abstract

This paper talks about the importance and usage of Java in both the mobile and non-mobile platforms. It further discusses the key aspects of Java which have revolutionized the concept of internet by providing dynamic web pages. This paper further argues evolution of Java that how it progressed and flourished for commercial usage. Afterwards, different versions of Java were created to support consumers of different levels. This paper further describes the features and the scope of Java in mobiles. Java platform for mobiles opened new horizons and offered various services to clients generating more revenue for operators and manufacturers. This paper further talks about Java mobile environment and its components especially CLDC which play vital role to run Java powered applications in mobile phones.

Introduction to Java:

Java is considered a unique language and many of its properties are also found in other languages. The extensive usage of Java language by programmers indicates that the Sun Microsystems have founded the right amalgam of sophistication and functionality. Java is actually derived from C++ language which increases the complexity of software with its features. However, the origin of Java is C++ and it uses many of its features by eliminating the drawback found in origin language. Java has eliminated direct memory access, pointers, multiple inheritance and pointers etc. Java was integrated with the support for World Wide Web and made it lucrative for the purpose of programming over network.

One of the main benefits which is associated with Java language is object orientation. Primitive languages such as Pascal, C and Basic are referred as procedural languages. These languages however offer the programming facilities to devise the software but they do not provide them in efficient way and do not provide robustness in nature. While Java devise software by keeping the concept of objects and classes under consideration. Classes contain the member of class along with the data and methods which further work upon the data. Java is actually object oriented in nature, however; there also exist many other object oriented languages such as Visual Basic, C++, Smalltalk and Delphi. (Reilly, Reilly, 2002)

Programmers happily adopt object oriented languages as they provide safety and ease as compared primitive procedural languages. One of the positive aspects of Java language is its simplicity as programmers refrain from using C++ due to complexity as it allows the direct memory access, dangling pointers and explicit memory de-allocation and allocation for structures and objects. Furthermore, Java supports inheritance but disallow the multiple inheritances. Java has been integrated with the automatic garbage collection which prevents the memory waste. In C and C++, the memory for structures and objects is allocated and after usage, memory is de-allocated otherwise the allocated memory may cause memory leakage.

Java satisfies the basic principles of object orientation such as encapsulation, inheritance, abstraction and polymorphism (Hunt, 2002) Java basically runs under the virtual environment which incorporates it in every operating system, this is why Java is compatible with Linux, Mac and Windows. Java incorporates the ability to run the code on every platform without the need recompilation again or changing in the source code. This aspect saves a lot time and amount as it alleviates the need to software creation for every platform.

The software which is created in Java supports every type of CPU and operating system with Java support. However, there is a cost which is associated with the portability feature as the source code of Java is converted into the bytecode which is further executed by Java Virtual Machine. This is why Java code does not run as fast as the native compiled code to instructions. However, when Just in Time special compiles is utilized for the conversion of java to native code but after conversion, it uses a lot of memory during operations.

Evolution of Java:

Java now has become on of the most establishment programming language and stands amongst the most adopted and famous programming languages. It is being utilized

4

nearly in every aspect of virtual world such as in applications for web hosts, desktops, enterprise systems and is also embedded in various devices such as Blu-ray players and mobile phones. (Parsons, 2012)

Java works with is virtual machine and Java runtime platform supports many other family languages such as Groovy, Scala, Python and Ruby. The beginning of Java was quite obscure and humble till its emergence by the means of web in 1995. It earned great repute in software development. It was a very humble beginning for java as it was invented by Sun Microsystems during the work on embedded systems for market. Sum Microsystems intended to develop this language for the development of software to empower the electronic consumer products i.e. PDA. After the completion of this project, it was further renamed to Oak which is actually a name of tree existed out side the project manager's window. (Reilly, Reilly, 2002)

These PDAs were based on microprocessors which further paved significant impact on electronic consumer devices. Sun Microsystems initially had started the internal research project which was named Green. However, this language later on resulted the C++ language but afterwards it was named as Oak language by the creator.(Deitel, 2009) During the period of domination of Oak, only Sun Microsystems were developing the applications swiftly. James Gosling is considered the father of Java language which actually emerged due to the modification of C++ compiler, but as result, new language emerged. There were many drawbacks were attached with C++ language which include runtime errors, memory leaks and cross pointers. But the new developed language was free from such disadvantages, however, very few disadvantages were found to be associated with the new born language.

With the passage of time, the paradigm was shifted from consumer electronic goods to online services hence the Oak team transferred their programming efforts to web browser and after that the name of language was changed to Hot java when it was first released in March 1995 as it also changed the perspectives of people using internet. With the advent technology of Java, it was made possible to create dynamic pages along with static pages at server end. Java applets were enabled to run on browsers and both the Netscape and Microsoft licensed this technology to make it compatible with their browser which further gave this language a great success.

Features of Java:

There exist numerous benefits which are considered responsible for the popularity of Java especially for internet. The very advantage of Java over internet is its capability to run applets. Applets are referred as tiny programs which easily incorporate with browser and run inside it. Before the advent technology of applets, web pages were static and Java bestowed them the dynamic property. Applets are tiny safe programs which dynamically run inside browser and cannot access hard disk; this property makes them safe and free from viruses. However, applets use the real potential of Java and also offer the support for graphical user interface (GUI). (Bhave, 2008)

A lot of features are associated with Java which distinguish it from other languages such as Java is simple than C++ as it has been alleviated with the need of pointers and operator overloading etc. The Java is most secure language as it involves the bytecode verifier, security manager and class loader along with removal of pointer usage. Java offers the portability feature as the code created in Java is written only once and can

6

be run anywhere. For this purpose, every platform owns its Java runtime machine. Java code can be written on any platform and the byte code generated can be run on any platform.

Java is basically an object oriented programming languages as the object and classes created can also be utilized again and again in other program, hence the object oriented programming in Java promotes the reusability. One of the great advantages of Java language is its robustness which prevents programs created in Java from crashing the platform. Microprocessors of current age work with very high speed and support multiple tasks at the same time. However, for a high speed single chip processor, multi tasks are acquired in Java with the help of multi-threading.

The ability to run multiple pieces of code at the same time is called multi-threading. Java is basically an interpreted programming language as when a program is written in Java, it is converted into class file which is also called the byte code. The interpreter hence executes the byte code. Java programming language does not depend upon specific architecture hence it can run on any microprocessor architecture, Java can run even on a microcomputer. The mobile phone now a day also runs java programs without any hassle. There are a lot of features integrated into Java makes this programming language comfortable in distributed systems. A java program can be easily written in lesser code as compared a program written in C++ language.

The code written in Java is much better than the code written in C++ due to the prevention of memory leaks by automatic garbage collection. As Java is object oriented, the code tested by other programmers can be easily integrated with the help of Java

Beans. The programs in Java language are written faster as compared to C++ due to inheritance and re-usability of already written and tested code.

Scope of Java in Mobiles:

According to Moore's law, the computer capabilities are doubled in every span of 18 months. In the meantime, prices of computer key components are dropped by halves. In this contemporary era, cheap processing devices are coupled with the devices for mobile communication and empowered the new generation to access the information at ease. According to International Data Corporation (IDC), most of workforce in U.S would be mobile workers. (Yuan, 2007)

There are many forces which affected the scope of Java ME in markets i.e. wireless operators, device manufacturers and consumers. The situation between wireless operators and device manufacturers is quite complex as there is often a huge competition seen with each other for the differentiation of their projects. (Rischpater, 2008) Device manufacturers are further categorized into two sub categories which are original equipment manufacturers and original design manufacturers. Original equipment manufacturers build and sell their products under their own label while the original design manufactures build and design the hardware to be sold under labels of others. There are countless wireless operators which heavily require Java ME runtime in phones which are provided to their consumers on their behalf. Now a day, operators are trying to find different ways to enhance their revenue and data services are considered one aspect for this purpose.

There are many java applications which totally rely over Java applications for contents. For many manufacturers, the provision of Java ME on devices is not just operator requirement from manufacturer's perspective. Java ME further enables the device manufacturers to bundle and create the applications for their devices in swift manner along with existed embedded toolkits. Java ME has also been adopted as one of the consumer requirements as it enhances the speed of product development along with the provision of differentiation opportunities along with the countless advantages over many other platforms.

Unlike Java Standard Edition, Java Enterprise Edition, Java Platform, Java ME has been crafted in manner to meet the power and cost constraints on small devices. Java ME application provides lucrative ways to operators in two ways i.e. driving of data and revenue generation in case of application distribution from operators. Such as you can easily purchase wallpaper or ring tones form the wireless portal of operators which further also provide Java applications for mobile as well. However, the partnerships between operators and developers enhance the communication channels for the boost of application sales and also bring revenue for both. For wireless telecommunication market, customers ask for usage ease, reliability and personalization.

According to Sun, two billions wireless terminals were sold in 2008 with the capability to run Java in initial java handset launch. Java platform enabled the devices for multimedia, communication and entertainment along with the support for application and customization for mobile users worldwide. Java in mobile enables the developers to offer freedom, choice and flexibility to subscribers. Furthermore, the basic platform not only allows developers to create stand alone applications but also allows them to devise games and network applications.

Java Environment in Mobile:

Cross-platform compatibility is considered one of the main reason for evolution of Java in mobiles (Yuan, 2004) Portability is accounted in case of similar hardware platforms or OSs. Currently, the scope of java is divided into three editions and each one has its own impact over mobility.

- Java 2 Standard Edition(J2SE): The base of Java of is J2SE as it further defines libraries and java virtual machines which are executed on workstations and standard PCs. For mobile devices, J2SE is considered an ample selection for wireless applications i.e. laptop-based.

- Java 2 Enterprise Edition (J2EE): This edition is in fact J2SE but it contains additional addons such as containers, serverside APIs and tools. This edition is intended to implement servers based on complex applications. The application servers of J2EE can effortlessly drive mobile applications which are based on browser i.e. xHTML and WML and can act as end points for services in smart mobile devices.

- Java 2 Micro Edition (J2ME): J2ME is designed especially for small devices. It is integrated with lightweight virtual machines which are designed in a special way and further embedded with minimal libraries as an alternate to standard libraries. J2ME is considered ideal for the development of mobile application especially for smart phone and PDAs.

10

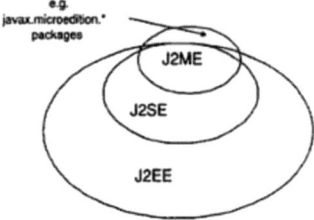

Figure 1: Architecture of Java 2 Platform

Similar architectures for application developed are followed in all java editions which ultimately reduce the cost without wastage of developer effort and further enhance the maintenance of products.

There come compatibility problems between J2ME and J2SE as there various types of mobile devise which have designed with varying features. We can say that the application which is developed for the automobile mounted system are found to be quite complex as compared to those which are intended for mobile phones. The compatibility issue is also observed on high end and low end devices as an application may use more resources in low end device. To cope with the issues aroused in terms of compatibility, J2ME has been integrated with various components such as profiles, configurations and optional packages.

To sort out the compatibility issue, each device needs a valid and specific combination of profile and configuration. The most generic and basic functionalities are offered by the means of configuration. The profile supports most advanced APIs and rests at the top of configuration. Theses advancements comprise of persistent storage,

11

graphical user interface, network connectivity and security. To support specific needs in application, further optional packages can be integrated with standard profiles.

Components of J2ME:

There are two components of J2Me which plays important role in terms of configuration. The very first configuration is known as Connected Limited Device Configuration (CLDC) which is intended for small devices with the memory of 160 KB or devices with a slow processor of 16 or 32 bit. The CLDC is limited in functions as it supports string, I/O function and math but lacks of Java Native Interface along with the custom class loaders. Only small numbers of class libraries are supported by the virtual machines of CLDC which are also known as Kilobyte Virtual Machines (KVM).

One of the latest versions of CLDC is 1.1 which has been released in March 2003 and was developed by JSR 139. The second component of J2ME is Connected Device Configuration (CDC) which supports the wireless devices with the memory of 2 MB and processors of 32 bit. It is quite different from CLDC as it offers the full features of Java 2 virtual machine and hence can easily take the advantage of J2SE libraries. The very first version of CDC was promulgated in March 2001 and developed by JSR 36.

Connected Limited Device Configuration (CLDC):

The concept of application is defined by CLDC which talks about the low level applications (Naing, 2008). It explains that it defines an application at basic level and Java Virtual Machine apprehends it as an executable code. CLDC is referred as the basic building block which is utilized to build J2ME profiles for pagers, cell phones and for low end palm devices. (Topley, 2002)

Java and the Mobile Environment

The devices are further categorized with respect to their processing power and memory resource limitations which prevents the utilization of full Java features. CLDC implements the java functions in a limited environment for the devices which have limited resources. CLDC makes java environment compatible with devices which are unable to run java with full features. For example, to run a simple application of "Hello World!" on the platform of windows, it requires the allocation of 16MB memory which is too much for small devices while in case of CLDC it requires 128 KB ROM or memory backed by battery to ensure the storage persistency of Java virtual machine along with class libraries.

For runtime allocation of 32 KB volatile memory is required to for the satisfaction of dynamic java applications which also include the heap allocation and class loading. To support the java runtime environment with the availability of limited resources, the reduced amount of requirements is specified by CLDC for language, core libraries and virtual machine. CLDC not only observes the restrictions for floating point but there are also some other features which are not incorporated with applications of CLDC. The reflection package is not available in CLDC just to save the memory. Similarly, due to shortage of memory, weak references are also not included. CLDC lacks of finalize() method as it produces greater complexities for very little outcome.

However, CLDC is integrated with the threading support but it does not offer the creation or production of daemon thread. CLDC has not been integrated with errors and exception handling system so when an error occurs, the device is urged to initiate the appropriate action instead of reporting.

13

Conclusion:

To conclude, Java has become essential for mobile phone manufacturers and operators at the same time. Operators and manufactures are trying to reap more and more lucrative benefits by unleashing the real power of Java by developing applications and utilities for mobile users. However, the current trend of Java is decreasing due to the advent technology of different mobile operating systems i.e. iOS, Android, and Bada OS. In this contemporary era, Android and iOS are being utilized most which do not support Java but they support applications made especially for them. But still many mobiles which are based on Symbian OS support Java. However, still the importance and vitality of Java mobile programming and applications cannot be neglected by consumers, operators and manufacturers.

References:

Bhave (2008), *Programming with Java*, New Delhi: Pearson Education India.

Deitel (2009), *Java For Programmers*, New Delhi: Pearson Education India.

Hunt, J. (2002) *Java and Object Orientation: An Introduction*. London: Springer.

Parsons, D. (2012). *Foundational Java Key Elements and Practical Programming*. London: Springer.

Rischpater, R. (2008) *Beginning Java ME Platform*. Berkeley, CA: Apress.

Reilly, D. (2002), and Michael Reilly. *Java Network Programming and Distributed Computing*. Boston, MA: Addison-Wesley.

Topley, K. (2002). *J2me in a nutshell*. New York: O'Reilly Media.

Yuan (2002), *Enterprise J2me : Dev Mobile Java Appl*, New Delhi: Pearson Education India.

Yuan, M. J. (2004) *Enterprise J2ME: Developing Mobile Java Applications*. Upper Saddle River, NJ: Prentice Hall PTR.